HIDEYUKI FURUHASHI

At last, we're diving into the final big event. This has been a wonderful series that's already run for far longer than expected, but I want to see the story through and do it justice!

BETTEN COURT

I had to keep doing the serialized chapters in the middle of a move to a new house, so preparing the content for this volume was tougher than it's ever been...

D0167479

VOLUME 12
SHONEN JUMP Edition

STORY: HIDEYUKI FURUHASHI
ART: BETTEN COURT
ORIGINAL CONCEPT: KOHEI HORIKOSHI

Translation & English Adaptation/Caleb Cook
Touch-Up Art & Lettering/John Hunt
Designer/Julian [JR] Robinson
Editor/Mike Montesa

VIGILANTE -BOKU NO HERO ACADEMIA ILLEGALS-
© 2016 by Hideyuki Furuhashi, Betten Court, Kohei Horikoshi
All rights reserved.
First published in Japan in 2016 by SHUEISHA Inc., Tokyo.
English translation rights arranged by SHUEISHA Inc.

The stories, characters, and incidents mentioned in this publication are entirely fictional.

No portion of this book may be reproduced or transmitted in any form or by any means without written permission from the copyright holders.

Printed in Canada

Published by VIZ Media, LLC
P.O. Box 77010
San Francisco, CA 94107

10 9 8 7 6 5 4 3 2 1
First printing, April 2022

MY HERO ACADEMIA VIGILANTES

12

Writer / Letterer
Hideyuki Furuhashi

Penciller / Colorist
Betten Court

Original Concept
Kohei Horikoshi

【charisma】

noun | cha • ris • ma
: a superhuman power or talent;
or : the ability to inspire admiration and devotion in others

CHARACTERS

[Vigilantes]

WANTED

POP☆STEP

(REAL NAME: KAZUHO HANEYAMA)

A self-styled freelance idol who gives impromptu live performances without the proper licensing or permits. Primary suspect in the Naruhata serial bombing case. Currently unconscious and receiving medical treatment for her grave condition.

WANTED

KNUCKLEDUSTER

(REAL NAME: UNKNOWN)

A middle-aged man of mystery who became the master Koichi never asked for. Though Quirkless, his fighting prowess is on par with pro heroes. Disappeared after the Sky Egg incident.

WANTED

THE CRAWLER

(REAL NAME: KOICHI HAIMAWARI)

A college senior and good-natured young man who started out his vigilante career under the moniker "Nice Guy," while making use of his Slide and Glide Quirk. Material witness in the Naruhata bombing case.

[Allies]

THE RAPPER

Brawler in the underground fighting club.

TIGER BUNNY

Mysterious bunny-eared high school girl.

SOGA KUGISAKI

Leader of a trio of ruffians in Naruhata.

MAKOTO TSUKAUCHI

Detective Tsukauchi's younger sister.

STORY

What is "justice" anyway? Get ready for a PLUS ULTRA spin-off set in the world of *My Hero Academia*!!

Heroes. The chosen ones who, with explicit government permission, use their natural talents, or Quirks, to aid society. However, not everyone can be chosen, and some take action of their own accord, becoming illegal heroes. What does justice mean to them? And can we really call them heroes? This story takes to the streets in order to follow the exploits of those known as *vigilantes*.

[Pro Heroes]

MIDNIGHT

THE SEXY, R-RATED HERO.

PRESENT MIC

THE VOICE HERO, WHO MAKES DECIBELS HIS WEAPON.

ERASER HEAD

THE ERASURE HERO, WHO APPROACHES EVERYTHING RATIONALLY.

ALL MIGHT

THE NUMBER ONE HERO AND SYMBOL OF PEACE.

INGENIUM

THE TURBO HERO BOASTS GODLIKE SPEED.

EDGESHOT

THE ENIGMATIC NINJA HERO.

BEST JEANIST

A SKILLED HERO WHO CONTROLS ALL FIBERS.

ENDEAVOR

THE FIERY NUMBER TWO HERO.

CAPTAIN CELEBRITY

A TOP HERO FROM THE U.S.A.

FAT GUM

A ROUGH AND TOUGH BRAWLING HERO FROM NAMIWA.

[Police]

EIZO TANUMA

A DETECTIVE UNRAVELING THE BIG PICTURE BEHIND THE DRUGS AND VILLAINS.

NAOMASA TSUKAUCHI

A DETECTIVE WHO'S FRIENDS WITH ALL MIGHT.

[Villains]

UNKNOWN

???????

KURORI

A VILLAIN WHOSE BODY CAN TRANSFORM INTO MIST.

NUMBER 6

THE SCARRED MAN WHO SCHEMES IN THE SHADOWS OF NARUHATA.

HOODED MAN

AN UNIDENTIFIED VILLAIN WHO SEEKS STRONG FIGHTERS.

MY HERO ACADEMIA VIGILANTES

12

CONTENTS

Ep. 92	Might Signal	007
Ep. 93	Three-Second Back-and-Forth	027
Ep. 94	Underground Roots	047
Ep. 95	Moon	067
Ep. 96	Negotiations	087
Ep. 97	Pursuers	109
Ep. 98	Irrational Persuasion Technique	131
Ep. 94.5	Tanuma's Report	153

EP. 92 - MIGHT SIGNAL
GLEAM
ALL MIGHT, INCOMING.
ROOF IS OPENING.
FWOO
FIVE SECONDS TO ALL MIGHT ARRIVAL.
ONE.
TWO.
WHOO
THREE.
FOUR.
OOOM

I AM HERE ...
BACK HOME !!
THUD!!
EP. 92 - MIGHT SIGNAL
YEAH

...BUT WHAT I DO WITH THE POWER *I WAS BORN WITH*...
...IS ONLY A SMALL FRACTION OF THE WORK THAT GETS DONE.
SHWP
SHWP
AHEM! MY STANCE IS THE SAME AS EVER!
THAT IS TO SAY, IT'S AN ABSOLUTE HONOR TO BE KNOWN AS THE *SYMBOL OF PEACE*...
CAN WE GET A COMMENT FROM THE SYMBOL OF PEACE HIMSELF?
STELLA WORK ALL MIGHT
YOU'VE SET A NEW RECORD FOR CONSECUTIVE INCIDENTS RESOLVED OVER THE PAST THREE DAYS.
ANYHOW, YOU HAVE MY THANKS, AS ALWAYS!
I KNOW WE'LL KEEP SUPPORTING EACH OTHER IN THE DAYS AND YEARS TO COME!
WHRRR
CLAP
CLAP
CLAP
CLAP
OOOH
YOU SEE, IT'S ALSO ALL THOSE OTHER HEROES—WITH THEIR OWN MYRIAD QUIRKS—WHO ARE OUT THERE PROTECTING OUR SOCIETY!
AS WELL AS YOU HARD-WORKING CIVILIANS!
WORMP
SHNK

EVEN IF THERE WERE ANY, I WOULD REFUSE THEM.
I'M READY FOR A SNOOZE, BUT...
...ANY MORE URGENT JOBS?
KCHK
GOING FOR 72 HOURS STRAIGHT CONSTITUTES SEVERE OVERWORK.
KLAK KLAK
YOUR ONLY URGENT MISSIONS NOW ARE REST AND RELAXATION.
HA HA... RIGHT YOU ARE.
DON'T YOU PUSH YOURSELF TOO HARD EITHER, OKAY?
TNK TNK TNK TNK TNK

LET'S JUST HOPE THAT THE WORLD REMAINS AT PEACE...
...FOR AT LEAST HALF A DAY STARTING NOW.
HMM ...?
TWITCH
FWP FWP FWP
I DON'T REQUIRE EXCUSES FROM YOU.
JUST GET SOME REST, ALL MIGHT.
KLAK KLAK
AH, NOT BECAUSE I NEED MY BEAUTY SLEEP OR ANYTHING. I JUST MEANT THAT WORLD PEACE...
...IS A GOOD THING, IN GENERAL.
COMING FROM... YES, OSAKA!
MIGHT EARS
AN EMERGENCY DISPATCH REQUEST!
BEEP!
TWNG
HRMM!
MIGHT SENSE

HAHAHA!
IT TURNED INTO ALL MIGHT!!
KASHING
L-LOOK.
RATTL
THAT AD...
IT'S MOVING...?
MIGHT SIGNAL
ALL MIGHT EMERGENCY PAGING SYSTEM (OSAKA)
HAHA HA HA!
HE'S ON HIS WAY!!
HE'S COMING!
RATTL
KASHING
!!
*KANI DOGE
*MIGHT
ALL MIGHT'S COMING HERE!!
ALL MIGHT
ALL MIGHT
ALL MIGHT
ALL MIGHT
CHATTER CHATTER

RR IP RR IP
THEY'RE CALLING ...
OSAKA ...
...IS...
ALLOW ME TO INQUIRE WHETHER OR NOT THERE ARE LOCAL HEROES WHO COULD RESPOND?
JUST A MOMENT, ALL MIGHT!
KLAK KLAK KLAK
...
...CALLING FOR ME!!
SHOO

RMMBL
RMMBL
SEEMS LIKE OUR BUNNY MADE HER ESCAPE.
WHICH MEANS ALL MIGHT IS BOUND TO SHOW UP...
...AND OUR JOB HERE IS DONE.
WHEN HE GIVES US AN OPENING, OU SHOULD RETREAT, FIND OMEWHERE TO HIDE, AND...
NAW.
I AIN'T HERE ON THE JOB.

...SO WHO WOULD I BE IF I DIDN'T INDULGE?
THAT PIECE O' WORK OVER THERE IS COMING FOR MY HEAD...
!
CLEARLY I UNDER-ESTIMATED HOW UNHINGED THIS GUY IS.
HELPING HIM LIVE TO SEE TOMORROW COULD BE TRICKY.

WOBBL WOBBL
FUN-FUN!!
Y...
YOU ...
...P-PEOPLE ...
YOU DOWN TO RUMBLE TOO?
YOU'RE MY KINDA GUY!!
SO NOW, THE QUESTION IS, CAN I FEND THIS THING OFF...
...UNTIL ALL'MIGHT GETS HERE?

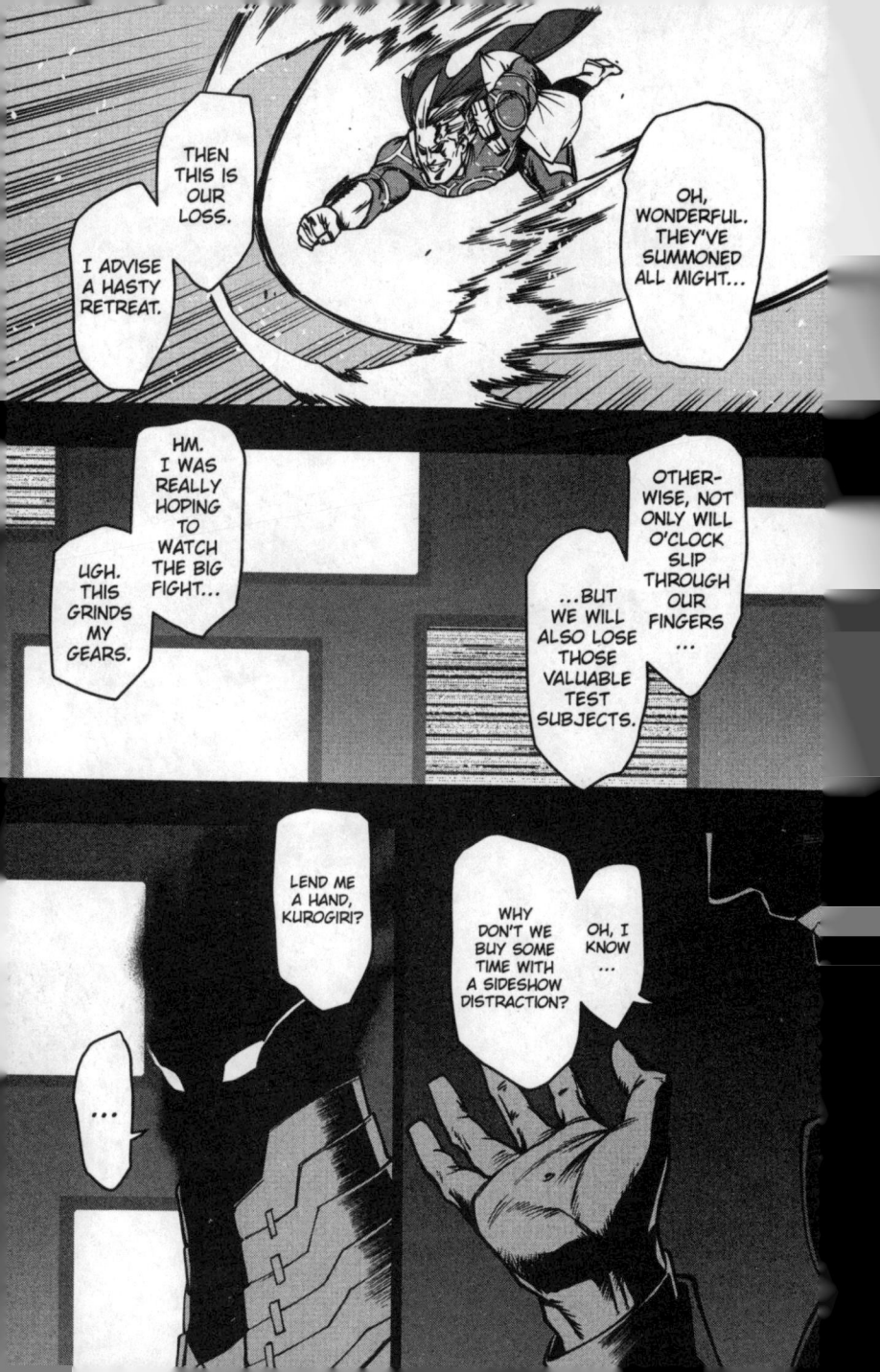
OH, WONDERFUL. THEY'VE SUMMONED ALL MIGHT...
THEN THIS IS OUR LOSS.
I ADVISE A HASTY RETREAT.
OTHER-WISE, NOT ONLY WILL O'CLOCK SLIP THROUGH OUR FINGERS ...
...BUT WE WILL ALSO LOSE THOSE VALUABLE TEST SUBJECTS.
HM. I WAS REALLY HOPING TO WATCH THE BIG FIGHT...
UGH. THIS GRINDS MY GEARS.
OH, I KNOW ...
WHY DON'T WE BUY SOME TIME WITH A SIDESHOW DISTRACTION?
LEND ME A HAND, KUROGIRI?
...

ZRM
ZRM
ZRM
ZRM
ZRM
ZRM
ZRM
ZRM
ZRM
ZRM
ZRM

YOU AND I MAY BE WHAT THE GOOD LITTLE CITIZENS AND POLITICIANS CALL VILLAINS...
KURO-GIRI...
...BUT WHAT IS A VILLAIN, REALLY?
THE TERM IS FAR TOO EMOTIONALLY CHARGED TO SIMPLY DESCRIBE A CERTAIN CLASS OF CRIMINAL, WOULDN'T YOU SAY?
IF THAT WERE ALL, WHY NOT JUST SAY "QUIRK CRIMINAL" AND BE DONE WITH IT?

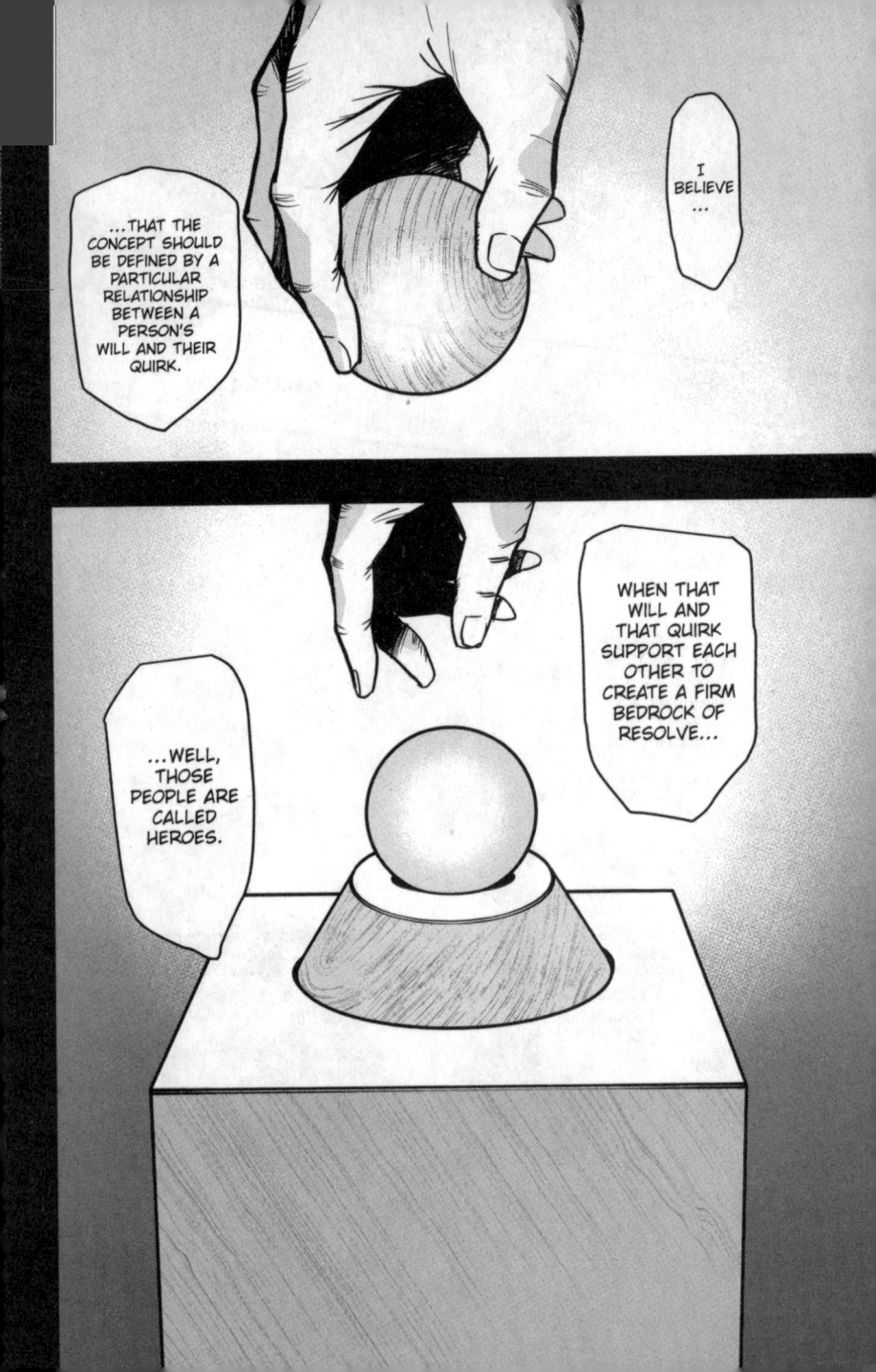
I BELIEVE ...
...THAT THE CONCEPT SHOULD BE DEFINED BY A PARTICULAR RELATIONSHIP BETWEEN A PERSON'S WILL AND THEIR QUIRK.
WHEN THAT WILL AND THAT QUIRK SUPPORT EACH OTHER TO CREATE A FIRM BEDROCK OF RESOLVE...
...WELL, THOSE PEOPLE ARE CALLED HEROES.

UNSTABLE CHARACTERS LIKE THAT...
...DEVIATE FROM THEIR PIGEONHOLES IN SOCIETY AND THREATEN TO DESTROY THE ENTIRE FRAMEWORK.
BUT WHEN AN EXTREME AND VIOLENT WILL STIMULATES A QUIRK INTO RUNNING AMOK...
...OR, ON THE FLIP SIDE, WHEN AN UNRULY QUIRK TWISTS A PERSON'S WILL TO ITS OWN ENDS...
...THAT DISPARITY CREATES A DANGEROUS IMBALANCE.
AS SUCH, THAT SORT OF LOGICAL EVIL OR ENEMY OF SOCIETY IS SHUNNED AND SCORNED...
...AS A VILLAIN.
...WHAT IS THE NEXT INEVITABLE CONCLUSION?
GOING BY THAT DEFINI-TION...
...THAT AT THE CORE OF VILLAINY IS THAT ESSENTIAL IMBALANCE.
MEANING ...

...LETTING ME TURN ANYONE INTO A VILLAIN.
BASICALLY, FORCING A PERSON'S QUIRK TO RAGE OUT OF CONTROL OR OTHERWISE FLIPPING THEIR QUIRK AROUND DESTROYS THAT BALANCE...
AW GEEZ, WHAT NOW ...?
RMMBL
WAHHH?!
THUM
POLICE

WHAAH
WHAT'S YOUR DEAL, HUH?!
RAA
RUMMBL
HA HA HA! WHAT DO YOU SAY TO THIS?
VILLAINS ARE SPILLING OUT INTO THE STREETS!
YA A A
DA HECK ?!
EVEN ALL MIGHT IS BOUND TO HAVE HIS HANDS FULL WITH THIS MESS.
SLA
I WONDER HOW LONG IT MIGHT TAKE HIM TO RESTORE THE PEACE?
DU DU DU
AEEE

YET... WE'VE GONE TOO FAR.
THIS INCIDENT WILL SURELY ...
...SERVE AS A CLUE THAT LEADS BACK TO US.
AND YOU'VE SIMPLY DROPPED IT IN THEIR LAPS.
GUILTY AS CHARGED.
THE POLICE, THOSE OTHER HEROES...
...AND ALL MIGHT HIMSELF ARE WELCOME TO IT.
H, MY LLOW!
Didn't mean to bring this!
SHOOM

NEVERTHE-LESS, I ACCEPT THAT RISK...
...IF IT MEANS I GET TO SEE O'CLOCK FIGHT.
HGAAA
KRAK KRAK
KRAKKRAKKRAK
AND IF AT ALL POSSIBLE, I WOULD LOVE TO GET MY HANDS...
WHOA! THIS THING'S PUMPING ITSELF UP, BIG-TIME!
HOW COULD THIS GET ANY BETTER?
...ON THAT PRECIOUS OVERCLOCK QUIRK OF HIS, HERE AND NOW.

SIR AND ALL MIGHT

Based on his design alone, Sir looks like someone who'd be amazing at paperwork, but an unintended consequence of that is the implication that All Might sucks at it by comparison.

That theory is sort of supported by evidence in the main series though.

—Furuhashi

I never imagined I'd get to draw Sir in *Vigilantes*. He was wearing a black suit in the flashback in the main series, so that's what I went with here.

I didn't have a chance to show his eyes behind the reflective glasses in the chapter, so here you go! (LOL)

—Betten

EP. 93 - THREE-SECOND BACK-AND-FORTH

SLAM
WE'VE GOT VILLAINS POURING OUTTA THAT PARKING STRUCTURE!
RUMMBL
THEY'RE INVADING THE NEARBY SHOPPING DISTRICT AND RESIDENTIAL AREAS!!
WAAAAH
NOW I GOT NO IDEA WHAT'S GOIN' ON HERE...
...BUT YOU VILLAINS AIN'T GETTIN' PAST ME!
ARGHHH!
RUMMBL

THERE'S GOING TO BE WIDESPREAD PANIC THROUGHOUT OSAKA!
ALL MIGHT'S GONNA HAVE HIS HANDS FULL WITH THIS!
GET DISPATCH REQUESTS TO LOCAL HEROES!
ZOOSH
MM-HMM!
I'VE GOT THE GIST!
1066
...
MIGHT INSIGHT
MIGHT EYES

SLAM
DASH!
SHAKI!
HAHAHA

Judo chop!
HAHA
HAHA
HAHA
YEAH
THUD

FWMP
AND ON THAT NOTE...
FWP FWP FWP FWP
FWP FWP
I AM HERE!
HOORAY! ALL MIGHT!
CLAP CLAP CLAP CLAP
WAAAA
POLICE POLICE POLICE POLICE POLICE POLICE POLICE

GOOD TO SEE YOU AGAIN, DETECTIVE TANUMA.
...I SUPPOSE THIS LITTLE CRISIS IS OVER?
I BELIEVE I'VE WRANGLED EVERY VILLAIN IN SIGHT, SO...
ERM... NOPE...
YOU DON'T SAY!
ALL MIGHT ONCE AGAIN LIVES UP TO EXPECTATIONS.
NEUTRALIZING SEVERAL DOZEN VILLAINS IN THE BLINK OF AN EYE...
WHY, THIS STUNT BARELY BOUGHT US ANY TIME AT ALL.
WRONG.
GRIN
IT BOUGHT US THREE SECONDS.

STARE
THIS HOODED MAN SOMEHOW REWORKED HIS BODY'S VERY STRUCTURE INTO A POWERHOUSE CAPABLE OF MASS DESTRUCTION.
HE'S TRANSFORMED FROM MARTIAL ARTIST TO MONSTER.
...MAKING HIM EASIER TO DEAL WITH.
SLAM
BUT WHEN HE PUMPS HIMSELF UP ALL JUMBO SIZED, HIS MOVES BECOME PRETTY UNINSPIRED...

...MY JOB IS TO BACK HIM UP WITH A BAG OF SUBTLE TRICKS.
AND NOW...
...WHILE RAPPER CHALLENGES THIS GUY TO A HEAD-ON FISTFIGHT...
RAHHHH!
OR SLICING HIS TENDONS WITH MY KNIFE.
LIKE SHOOTING OUT THE ENEMY'S EYES WITH A PISTOL.
OR TACKLING HIM, TO KNOCK HIM OFF-BALANCE.
RABABABABAM

THEN WHEN I'M OUTTA STEAM, I LET RAPPER COVER ME...
...SO I CAN TAKE A BREATHER AND...
!!
RAPPER!
SLAM!

HE... GRABBED PART OF THE CAGE FROM THE RING?
SKRRCH
STRIKING FROM ABOVE WITH A MAKESHIFT FLYSWATTER!
HE'S USING HIS HEAD...
FWSH
NO WAY TO DODGE!
HNGH

DID SOME-ONE ORDER ...
...A GOOD KICK-ING ?!
BAM!
THB
FWP FWP FWP

WHY'D YOU COME BACK, BUNNY?!
SKFSH
YOU AGAIN!
AND I WASN'T GONNA BE THE ONLY GAL ON THE SIDELINES.
...I FINISHED YOUR LITTLE FAVOR.
OUT THERE, IN HERE–IT'S TOTALLY NUTS.
CUZ...
BUNNY? MORE LIKE A MAD DOG!
GRR
SO I'M BACK TO GIVE THIS NASTY CUSTOMER A TASTE OF MY FOOT!!

GRAA A H
KRKKRKKRAK
SNAPOP
Y-YOU TH-THREE ...
K-KILLING YOU...
... STRON-GEST.
... WOULD M-MAKE ME...
KK

THE HELL WITH THAT !!
YOU'D BETTER RETREAT, BUNNY.
SNEAK ATTACKS WON'T CUT IT NOW.
YEAH. SCRAM.
THINK WHAT YOU WANT, BUT I'M A HERO IN TRAINING, SEE?
I'M NOT GONNA TURN TAIL WHEN THERE'S A VILLAIN BEGGING FOR A BEATING!
TCH.
BUT... SHE DID HER JOB WELL.
GLANCE
OH BOY. ANOTHER WILD CHILD TO BABYSIT?
HEY, BUB. WHAT DO WE DO ABOUT THE CRAZY CHICK?
...

I...
...A
A
A
AA
M...

THE FEW SECONDS SHE BOUGHT US...
...GAVE HIM TIME TO SHOW UP.

ZRM
OUR TIME IS UP.
I WILL RETRIEVE THE SUBJECT.
!
?!
R
ZRRM
I CAN STILL F-
W- WAIT!
ZRM ZRM

FIWF
ZRM
... FIGHT ...
... HERE !!
BUH
HUH?
THE VILLAIN GOT AWAY.
!
SEE THAT, BUB?
THAT BIG MONSTER THING WENT POOF!

HOOD

I was glad I decided to bring in the brawler who eventually becomes the Nomu called Hood and just have him wearing a sweatshirt with a hood. (LOL) But if that had been the extent of it, people might've been like, "Wait, who was that anyway?" so we needed to have him grow gigantic, as an extra hint.

—Furuhashi

Horikoshi Sensei went out of his way to provide us with concept art for a midway point of Hood's evolution, but the timing just didn't work out right on our end. Sorry!

—Betten

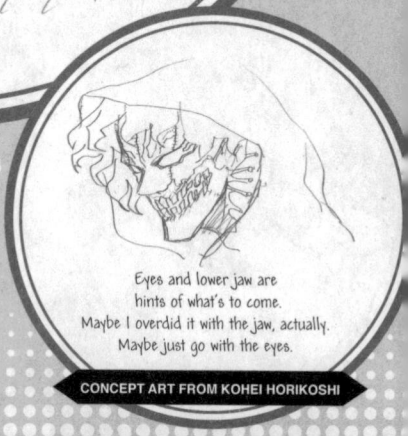

CONCEPT ART FROM KOHEI HORIKOSHI

EP. 94 - UNDERGROUND ROOTS

THE MASS OUTBREAK OF VILLAINS THAT THREATENED OSAKA'S SUPER MINAMI DISTRICT...
...WAS DEALT WITH IN A FLASH BY THE HEROIC EFFORTS OF ALL MIGHT, WHO DASHED ON TO THE SCENE!!
WOO
YEAH ALL MIGHT!
ALL MIGHT MANAGED TO PUT A STOP TO NEARLY 100 VILLAINS IN ONE FELL SWOOP...
...WHICH NOW STANDS AS A NEW RECORD FOR THE HERO.
HE DID IT ALL, INCLUDING RESCUING THE INJURED, REINFORCING DAMAGED BUILDINGS, AND CLEARING AWAY RUBBLE.
THE NUMBER ONE HERO NEVER SLACKS ON THE JOB!
FAREWELL, CITIZENS!
SHOOK

FOOM
MIGHT SLEEP
Zzz...
NOM NOM
NO DECENT HERO SHOULD GET SHOVED AROUND BY VILLAINS, YEAH?
MAYBE PUTTING ON SOME WEIGHT WOULD WORK FOR ME TOO.
NANIWA
YOU GOT IT, PAL!!
TEN MORE BOXES, MA'AM!!
SLAM
SIGH... NO DENYIN' IT—THAT ALL MIGHT'S A BIG DEAL.
It's Fat!
WORM
Yay!

RAAAAAAAGH
ZSH
CRAASHH!
KRAK
KRAK KRAK
KZZT KZZT
FOOM
I-I... CAN STILL FIGHT!
F-FIGHT !!

NO.
WH
AM
WSH
?!
KRK
KRK
AFTER JUST A FEW MINUTES OF BATTLE ...
...YOUR STRENGTH, AGILITY, AND REGENERATION HAD TAKEN A NOSEDIVE.
YOU'RE FAR FROM BEING A PRACTICAL PAWN.
TH

YOUR COMMITMENT TO BRAWLING IS A WORTHY TRAIT, BUT...
I THOUGHT YOUR MARTIAL ARTS WOULD GET THE JOB DONE, BUT I MISSED THE MARK THERE.
What a letdown.
...IT MESHES POORLY WITH YOUR NEW SHAPE-SHIFTING ABILITY.
BULKING UP FROM THE VERY START MIGHT'VE BEEN THE BEST WAY TO CRUSH THEM, ACTUALLY.
...
...
ZRM ZRM
...
THE MODIFICATIONS WILL TAKE TIME AND EFFORT.
SEND THAT ONE OVER TO THE DOCTOR FOR ME.
VERY WELL.

...LEADS ME CLOSER TO HIM.
...SINCE ALL OF THIS... EVERY STEP...
STILL, NO CAUSE FOR ALARM. I CAN BE PATIENT...
KREEK
...IS A RARE AND WONDROUS ABILITY.
INDEED. THE ACCELERATION OF MENTAL ACTIVITY PROVIDED BY OVER-CLOCK...
STILL, GETTING MY HANDS ON THAT ONE QUIRK WOULD HAVE FURTHERED THE CAUSE...
I'VE EVEN DECIDED HOW I'LL PUT IT TO USE.
YES.
AND IT WILL BE MINE, EVENTUALLY.

SEEMS LIKE THE ACTION'S ALL OVER.
I'D BETTER MOVE ALONG.
KEEP OUT
POLICE
GOOD WORK TODAY.
YOU KNOW, THE COPS MIGHT JUST TOSS SOME COMPENSATION YOUR WAY IF I MENTION YOU IN THE OFFICIAL REPORT.
THEY CAN KEEP IT.
I'LL BE RAKING IT IN ON MY OWN BEFORE LONG.
AND THE NEXT TIME WE BUMP INTO EACH OTHER...
...I'LL PROLLY BE A FULL-BLOWN HERO.
HOW 'BOUT YOU, PUNCH-MAN?

...TO SAVE MY LESS DEADLY KICKS FOR GUYS LIKE YOU.
ME BEING ME'S THE ONLY WAY I KNOW.
I DUNNO ...
FWAH
A VILLAIN HUH?
WELP, I'LL BE SURE...
TIP

I'D BEST GET A MOVE ON TOO.
SHWP
WE SMASHED UP MY PLAY-GROUND REAL GOOD...
...BUT THERE'RE PLENTY OF OTHER CLUBS OUT THERE.
KEEP IN MIND YOU'RE PLAYING WITH FIRE.
THE UNDER-GROUND MASQUERADE WAS JUST THE TIP OF THE ICEBERG. A FRONT.
I'VE GOT NO DOUBT THAT THEY'LL CHANGE THE NAME AND GET IT BACK UP AND RUNNING ELSEWHERE.
AND IF WE SEE A REPEAT OF WHAT WENT DOWN TODAY...
WELL, YOU MIGHT NOT MAKE IT OUT ALIVE NEXT TIME.
YEAH? I CAN'T WAIT.
RIP
FWP
HERE'S WHAT *YOU* OUGHTA KNOW IF WE CROSS PATHS AGAIN...

NEXT TIME, I'M PLAYING FOR KEEPS.
THE NEXT DAY
MY OVERCLOCK IS BETTER SUITED TO INTEL GATHERING THAN STRAIGHT-UP COMBAT.

HA
HA
HA
HA
THAT'S BEEN MY USUAL ROUTINE UP TO NOW. IT'S MY BREAD AND BUTTER...
...AND WHEN THERE'S PROPER EVIDENCE, I'LL LOOP IN THE AUTHORITIES AND OTHER HEROES.
I'LL FOLLOW THE TRAIL SOLO UNTIL I GET A GOOD LEAD...
AND I HAD TO RECRUIT A PAIR OF ACCOMPLICES IN THE FIELD.
BUT THIS TIME, SOME UNEXPECTED INTERFERENCE SHOWED UP.
...THEY'RE SURE TO KEEP AN EYE ON OUR COMINGS AND GOINGS.
THIS ENEMY IS CRAFTY.
NOW THAT WE'RE HOT ON THEIR TRAIL...
THERE'S A GOOD CHANCE THEY'LL OUTSMART WHATEVER YOU TOSS AT THEM THROUGH OFFICIAL CHANNELS.
SORRY, BUT I'M ASKING YOU TO LET ME KEEP INVESTIGATING AS I SEE FIT, AT MY DISCRETION.
YEAH...? I DON'T SUPPOSE YOU WANNA DIVULGE ANY INFO TO US...
...ABOUT THAT INTERFERENCE? OR THOSE ACCOMPLICES?

IS THIS JUST YOU BEING CAUTIOUS ...?
BEING CAUTIOUS AND VIGILANT, YES.
BUT SOMETIMES, CAUTION ALONE ISN'T ENOUGH.
THERE'S PLENTY ELSE I NEED TO TACKLE A CASE LIKE THIS.
AUDACITY.
DIVERSITY.
FREEDOM.
ALL IN ALL...
HEH
MAYBE?
IMAGI-NATION ?
?
I'LL BE IN TOUCH.

PRESENT DAY

EMPTY

I COULD USE ANOTHER CUP TOO.
I'M GOING FOR A COFFEE REFILL, TANUMA, SIR.

...BUT THAT UNDERGROUND MASQUERADE CASE TURNED OUT TO BE A THREAD CONNECTED TO THE BADDEST OF ALL THE BAD GUYS.
O'CLOCK WASN'T WILLING TO SPILL TOO MANY DETAILS WHEN IT ALL WENT DOWN...
...
WHICH ALL GOT SOLVED THROUGH THAT SECRET SHOWDOWN BETWEEN HIM AND ALL NIGHT, BEHIND THE SCENES...

THEN, THE RASH OF INSTANT VILLAIN CASES IN NARUHATA...
FIRST, THE UNDERGROUND MASQUERADE CASE...
BUT I'M HAVING DÉJÀ VU...

THEN, WE HAD THAT BUSINESS AT THE SKY EGG.
THE CHAIN OF EVENTS IN NARUHATA STARTED WITH THOSE REMODELED VILLAINS, WHO MOSTLY GOT USED FOR TERRORISM...
AND I'M THINKING THOSE RECENT BOMBINGS IN DOWNTOWN NARUHATA MIGHT JUST BE CONNECTED TOO.

OH, THAT WAS QUICK.
TANUMA? SIR?
COULD BE THE SAME MYSTERY ORGANIZATION BEHIND THE MASQUERADE...
THE SAME MASTERMIND, EVEN...

OOPS... WHO'RE YOU AGAIN?
ERM ...
SURE THING.
TAP TAP
COULD I CHECK OVER WHAT YOU REMOVED ?
I WORK OVER IN THE ARCHIVES.
THERE'S A PROBLEM WITH THE PAPERWORK YOU SUBMITTED WHEN YOU SIGNED OUT THOSE DOCUMENTS.
SO I'M GONNA NEED TO HANG ON TO THESE FILES A LITTLE LONGER.
...TO THE VILLAIN OUTBREAKS IN NARUHATA OVER THE PAST FEW YEARS.
I'M IN THE MIDDLE...
...OF TYING OSAKA'S OLD UGM CASE...

?!
BOOM
NO, I'M AFRAID I HAVE TO PROCESS THEM NOW.
...SINCE IT WOULD DREDGE UP PLENTY OF OTHER NASTY BUSINESS.
SEE, YOUR DRAWING A LINE BETWEEN THIS, THAT, AND THE OTHER THING WOULD BE A REAL HEADACHE ...
DOOM
BOOM
KK
WHO THE HELL ARE YOU ?!

BOOOMM!!
TMP
ZSH
SKF
ZSH
THAT'S A JOB WELL DONE, NUMBER 6.

KEEP THE ENEMY IN THE DARK...
BOM
WITHOUT THE PROPER INFORMATION, THE POWERS THAT BE CAN'T MAKE A MOVE.
ALWAYS STRIKE FIRST...
...TO ERASE EVERY TRACE OF THE PAST.
FWAH
NO DOUBT, MASTER. ♪
PLP
PLP
PLP
...TO REMAIN FREE...
...AND UNTOUCH-ABLE.
O
O
O
M

KENDO RAPPA'S FACE REVEAL

The idea of the goofy masked man actually being kind of handsome was just too perfect. So when I heard that the anime offered a glimpse of his face (and he turned out to be good-looking), I thought, "Ooh, lucky us."

—Furuhashi

I went to check the video when I learned about Rappa's partial face reveal in the anime, but it's such a brief moment that I had to keep rewinding in my attempts to pause it perfectly. (LOL)

—Betten

EP. 95 - MOON
KLAK KLAK KLAK
YO, ERASER! WORKING AFTER HOURS AGAIN? YOU SURE GOT PASSION FOR THE JOB!
BUT WHADDAYA SAY WE GRAB SOME GRUB?
YEAHHHHHH!
YEAH?
NO THANKS.
FW
R
R
RL
SHWP
SHWP
I'M SUBBING FOR MIDNIGHT, AND HER WORK'S BEEN PILING UP.
KLAK
KLAK
WHAT COULD SHE BE THINKING ...
... LEAVING HER KIDS IN THE LURCH.

MY SENSITIVE EARS CAN'T TAKE IT ANYMORE!
AFTER THE BREAK, WE'LL HAVE MORE NARUHATA NEWS FOR YOU.
YOU GOTTA GET BETTER EARBUDS, DUDE. THESE'VE GOT SERIOUS SOUND LEAKAGE.
SAY, WHATCHA LISTENING TO OVER HERE? HMM?
SHWP
NOT REALLY.
SINCE SOME PALS OF YOURS GOT CAUGHT UP IN THAT WHOLE MESS.
GUESS YOU'RE FRETTING 'BOUT THE TROUBLE OVER IN NARUHATA, HUH?
SADLY ...
I MEAN, IF YOU CARE THAT MUCH, YOU COULD KEEP WIPING THEIR BUTTS FOR 'EM.
YOU HAD TO SEE IT COMING THOUGH, YEAH?
IT WAS ALWAYS GONNA TURN OUT LIKE THIS FOR THOSE SORTA FOLKS ...

...I'M NOT THEIR TEACHER.
HAH! GOOD ONE!
LIKE I JUST SAID, MY EARS ARE SHARP.

YOU CAN TRY TO HIDE IT BEHIND THAT GRUMPY MUG...
...BUT THE TRUTH COMES OUT IN YOUR VOICE.
...

THEN I'D BETTER KEEP QUIET.
YOU CAN SHUT UP TOO.
SEE WHAT I MEAN?
WRONG.
WRONG.
SUCH A DECENT GUY, BUT TRYING SOOO HARD TO BE A STICK-IN-THE-MUD.
DING

GOT A TEXT?
WHO'S IT FROM?

DETECTIVE TSU-KAUCHI ...

EP. 95 - MOON

THE DOCTORS AREN'T SURE WHEN SHE'LL REGAIN CONSCIOUSNESS EITHER...
ABOUT POP'S CONDITION... SHE'S STABLE FOR NOW, BUT...
...THE PHYSICAL TRAUMA SHE EXPERIENCED MEANS SHE'S NOT OUT OF THE WOODS YET.
I HAVE TO ASK...
DO YOU BOYS INTEND TO COOPERATE WITH THE AUTHORITIES?
SURE... I'LL GIVE 'EM ALL THE INTEL THE OLD FART COLLECTED.

BUT ONLY ONCE POP'S SAFETY IS GUARANTEED.
I WANT THEM GUARDING HER ROUND THE CLOCK, YOU HEAR ME?
YEAH. GOT IT.
YOU BOYS BE CAREFUL, OKAY? DON'T BITE OFF MORE THAN YOU CAN CHEW.
BEEP
YES, WE CAN'T AFFORD TO GET CARELESS... ESPECIALLY WHEN THE POLICE STATION WAS JUST ATTACKED.
I'VE EVEN HAD POP'S MOTHER LEAVE THE HOSPITAL, FOR NOW.
YOU STILL HANGING OUT UP THERE, KOICHI?
UM, YEAH. NOTHING NEW TO REPORT ...
BUT TO BE TOTALLY HONEST, WEARING THE SAME UNDERPANTS FOR THIS LONG IS KINDA GROSS.
DID WE REALLY NEED TO KNOW THAT?
RAPT! GET THE MAN A CHANGE OF CLOTHES.
HERE'S THE KEY TO HIS PLACE.
SURE!

UNDERPANTS, SHIRT, SOCKS, TOWEL... RIGHT.
UNDER-PANTS, SHIRT, SOCKS, TOWEL ...

WHAT A DUMP!
HOW CAN THE GUY LIVE IN A PLACE LIKE THIS?

HANG ON NOW.
HUH?
IS THAT WINDOW OPEN?

BURGLARS?
S'NOT LIKE IT'S MY PLACE!
WELL, WHAT-EVS!
GYAH HAH!
...
UMM... UNDER-PANTS, SHIRT...
AND WHAT ELSE, AGAIN?

CAPTAIN
POP, POP! CHECK IT OUT!
HMM? WHAT IS IT?
THE MOON'S REAL PRETTY TONIGHT.
OH, YOU'RE RIGHT!
...
WAIT, IS THAT ALL?
WELL... MY BUILDING'S SHORTER THAN THE OTHERS AROUND HERE.
SO THE VIEWS AREN'T GREAT.

TRUE. WE'RE BOXED IN BY ALL THESE WALLS...
BUT...
...A SMALLER SLICE OF SKY MAKES THE MOON LOOK BIGGER.
WHICH IS A-OK IN MY BOOK.
...
WOW. THAT'S LIKE...
...SOOO DEEP.
AW, C'MON.
I THOUGHT IT WAS A COOL LINE!!
LET'S CALL IT FOLKSY. AND THAT'S ME BEING GENEROUS.

THERE'S ANOTHER PRETTY MOON OUT TONIGHT.
HEY, POP.
...WE'LL HAVE PLENTY TO TALK ABOUT.
ONCE YOU'RE ALL BETTER...

THE SMALL STUFF. THE SILLY STUFF.
THE STUFF THAT MAKES LIFE JUST A LITTLE MORE FUN.
WE'LL TALK UNTIL WE'RE ALL TALKED OUT.

AND I KNOW THAT MIGHT NOT BE AS SOON AS WE'D LIKE, BUT...

I'M NOT GOING ANYWHERE.
...THAT'S OKAY.

THE SAME MOON'S LOOKING DOWN ON US BOTH.

特別警戒中
ENOUGH OF THAT, ALREADY!
*HIGH ALERT STATUS
MY POLICE WORK IS NOT UP FOR CASUAL DISCUSSION! AM I MAKING MYSELF CLEAR?!
GEEZ, JUST MAKING SMALL TALK.
LOOK, I KNOW YOU TOLD ME NOT TO BRING UP THE PEOPLE INVOLVED IN THOSE CASES ...
...SO ALL I'M DOING IS ASKING MY MAN ON THE SCENE HOW THE OLD NEIGHBOR-HOOD'S DOING.
LOVELY. STRAIGHT BACK TO YOUR OLD M.O.
WE'RE DONE TALKING.
ANY NEWS FROM YOUR BROTHER ?
HE'S BEING ESPECIALLY CAGEY, AS I EXPECTED.
THE INVESTI-GATION MUST NOT BE GOING TOO WELL.
I'LL JUST HAVE TO KEEP DOING MY PART, IN THE MEAN-TIME.
KLAK KLAK

THE BOMB AT THE STATION THE OTHER DAY...
...WAS CLEARLY PART OF A PLOT TO HINDER THE NARUHATA INVESTIGATION.
SIGH...
I HATE TO ADMIT IT, BUT IT FEELS LIKE SOGA KUGISAKI WAS RIGHT...
WHO THE HELL ARE YOU ?!
OH? THOSE BODIES ARE WEIGHING ON YOU?
MAYBE IF YOU PEOPLE COULD ACTUALLY DO YOUR JOBS RIGHT...
AND NOW TANUMA IS IN CRITICAL CONDITION AND SHOWING NO SIGNS OF WAKING UP.
THEY'RE NOT EVEN SURE HE'LL PULL THROUGH.
?!
BAM
DETEC-TIVE...

WHAT CAN I DO FOR YOU, SANSA?
AH... SORRY. JUST MULLING THINGS OVER...
ERM, WHAT?

GOOD.
FWP

...FOR KOICHI HAIMAWARI, A.K.A. THE CRAWLER.
IT'S JUST ARRIVED.
THE ARREST WARRANT ...

...AS THE AUTHORITIES, WE CAN'T ALLOW OURSELVES TO RELY ON OUTLAWS.
"VIGILANTISM IS A BACKUP PLAN FOR WHEN OFFICIAL LAW AND ORDER INSTITUTIONS FALL SHORT."
TO DO SO WOULD BE TO ADMIT THAT THE JUSTICE SYSTEM HAS FAILED.
THERE MAY BE A GRAIN OF TRUTH TO THAT IDEA, BUT...

I'VE LET THESE "GOOD SAMARITANS" RUN AMOK FOR THIS LONG, BUT NOW IT HAS TO END.
THE OPERATION WE'VE TALKED ABOUT?
LET'S GET STARTED THEN.
KNOW THIS, VIGILANTES OF NARUHATA ...
I'M TAKING BACK THE REINS NOW.

THE COPS

I've gotten lots of feedback about Sansa along the lines of "cute kitty cat ♪" but he's no spring chicken, actually. He's a full-grown adult. Tsukauchi is also in his thirties.

And Tanuma is genuinely deserving of being called "old dude."

—Furuhashi

Sansa is visually striking, but we have basically no other info about him. Which led to lots of moments while drawing where I was like, "Eh, this is probably fine, I guess?"

—Betten

EP. 96 - NEGOTIATIONS

UM, HELLO...
ANY WORD ON WHAT HAPPENED WITH POP AFTER ALL THAT?
MEOW
MORE OF US? WHAT'S THAT MEAN?
OH... MORE OF YOU, HUH?
AH.
PARDON ME, I WAS TOLD TO INQUIRE ABOUT POP HERE AT HOPPERS...
Ah... More of us...

AND APPARENTLY THE CRULLER IS OUT THERE DOING ALL HE CAN.
MISS POP'S NOT GETTING WORSE, BUT SHE'S NOT GETTING BETTER EITHER.
ACCORDING TO MIDNIGHT ...
WE'LL GET THE WORD OUT IF THERE'S AN UPDATE...
...SO GO HOME AND GET BACK TO STUDYING.
MIDNIGHT ALSO SAID YOU KIDS SHOULDN'T WORRY YOURSELVES SICK...

...
OF COURSE... WE DON'T WANT TO INTRUDE ON YOUR BUSINESS.
LET'S ALL CALL IT A DAY, OKAY?

FWP

WELL, SINCE YOU'RE ALREADY HERE...
...WHY NOT HAVE A BITE TO EAT?
IT'S ON THE HOUSE THIS TIME.
Menu
Harper's Cafe

*UNDER CONSTRUCTION

USE THIS ONE TO GET IN TOUCH.
I'M CARRYING TWO PHONES NOW.
THAT'S WHAT HE TOLD ME.
Personal phone
I ONLY TURN ON MY OLD PHONE ONCE A DAY.
LET'S SEE...
AH?
A MILLION MISSED CALLS FROM MOM.
Ugh...
They talked once after the incident.
TEXTS FROM DAD?
What's going on?
Need help with anything?

...
Got it.
BEEP
Phew...
BEEEP
BEEP
All good here.
BEEP
We'll talk once things calm down.
Take care of Mom.
TAP TAP
I'LL BE RIGHT OVER!
WAIT, NO!
GONNA TOSS IT!
OH? COOL.
HEYYY!
GOT FOOD, KOICHI!

BOOF
HUP!

EH?
OH ...
YOU'RE JUST FLYING ALL OVER THE PLACE NOW, HUH?

I'M KINDA OVER IT ALREADY.

HOW'S IT LOOKING DOWN ON THE GROUND?
THE WHOLE STAKEOUT THING, EVERY DAY. AND THEY GOT ME RUNNING ERRANDS.
SAME OLD, SAME OLD.

GYA-HAH!
WHERE IS SOGA? I DIDN'T SEE HIM DOWN THERE.
NOT THAT I'LL ADMIT IT.
SOGA'D GET MAD AND BE ALL, "GET A GRIP."
SO SERIOUS, THAT PUNK.
I TOLD HIM THERE'D BEEN A BREAK-IN...
...SO HE WANTED TO CHECK IT OUT.
LEAVING ME ALONE? REALLY...?
HE'S OVER AT YOUR PLACE, ACTUALLY.
A BREAK-IN?!
NO ONE TOLD ME!
AT MY PLACE ?!
OH, RIGHT ...
"IT'LL JUST BE A DISTRACTION FOR KOICHI, SO DON'T TELL HIM."
That's what he said.
SURE... NOW'S NOT THE TIME TO WORRY ABOUT THAT ANYHOW.
AND BESIDES–I'VE GOT NOTHING WORTH STEALING.
IT'S A SECRET, 'KAY?

SO KOICHI'S THE ONLY RENTER LEFT IN THIS OLD BUILDING.
THEY'RE BUYING UP PROPERTY LEFT AND RIGHT AROUND HERE, WITH PLANS TO REDEVELOP THE WHOLE AREA.
TAP
BUT THERE'S NO SIGN THAT THEY RAN-SACKED THE ROOM.
THE PERP BROKE THE GLASS AND GOT INSIDE THROUGH THE WINDOW.
THE PLACE IS BASICALLY ABANDONED.
NOT A LIKELY TARGET FOR YOUR AVERAGE SNEAK THIEF.
THEY MUST'VE COME FOR SOMETHING SPECIFIC.

KRZZK
BASED ON THE DUST PATTERN, SOMEONE'S BEEN IN AND OUT OF THERE...
MAYBE JUST BULKY TRASH, LEFT BEHIND BY THE LAST OCCUPANT?
SOMETHING'S STASHED OVER IN THE CORNER OF THIS EMPTY SPACE.
NO... LOOKS LIKE IT WAS BROUGHT IN RECENTLY.
GRP
!!
PRRRR!

TH-THEY'RE HERE...
SOGA ...
MOYURU? WHAT'S UP?
TMP
THE COPS!
TMP
BAM
POLICE
POLICE
POLICE

!
SOGA KUGISAKI!
STARTING TODAY, WE'LL BE IN CHARGE OF SECURITY FOR THIS HOSPITAL WARD.
NO COMPLAINTS FROM YOU, I ASSUME?
AND AS WITNESSES TO THE SERIAL BOMBINGS, YOU'RE GOING TO COOPERATE WITH OUR INVESTIGATION.
YOU BOYS IN BLUE ARE BEEFING UP SECURITY?
YEAH, COURSE I'M FINE WITH THAT.
I'M JUST A CIVILIAN, AFTER ALL...
...SO IF THE PROS WANNA DO THEIR JOBS, I'M DOWN.
BUT...

YOU PEOPLE SURE DRAGGED YOUR FEET BEFORE MAKING THIS MOVE.
HONESTLY, TOO SLOW FOR MY TASTE.
...
PLUS, IT COULD TAKE WEEKS... MAYBE EVEN MONTHS FOR POP TO MAKE A FULL RECOVERY.
ARE YOU PREPARED TO DEVOTE YOUR RESOURCES FOR THAT LONG?
WELL, ERM...
SURE, SURE. YOU GOT YOUR RULES AND REGULATIONS, I KNOW.
AND IT'S NOT LIKE YOU CAN SPARE INFINITE RESOURCES...
...ON A SINGLE GIRL WHO'S GETTING THE VILLAIN TREATMENT TO BOOT.
WHICH IS WHY I AIN'T PREPARED TO HAND OVER THE REINS COMPLETELY.
YOU COPS ARE SET UP TO KEEP THE PEACE IN GENERAL.
AND SURE-I CAN'T DENY THAT'S A WORTHY CAUSE.
BUT YOUR BIG OL' SYSTEM AIN'T MADE...
...TO CATCH STUFF THAT FALLS THROUGH THE CRACKS.

STP
KUGISAKI ...
I DON'T DISAGREE, WHICH IS WHY WE'VE GOT TO HAVE EACH OTHER'S BACKS IN ALL THIS.
SORRY, BUT THIS ISN'T UP FOR DEBATE. NOT ANYMORE.
TRY TO COOPERATE WITH THE POLICE FOR NOW...
...AND LATER WE CAN DISCUSS A LONG-TERM SECURITY PLAN...

KOICHI HAIMAWARI, A.K.A. "THE CRAWLER" ...
HE'S WANTED FOR REPEATED UNAUTHORIZED QUIRK USE, AND WE'VE GOT A WARRANT FOR HIS ARREST.
GIVING HIM THE VILLAIN TREATMENT TOO, HUH?

YOU DON'T THINK HE'S PREPARED FOR THAT?
WHICH COULD LEAD TO A BATTLE.
HE'S GIVEN US NO CHOICE.
LEFT TO HIS OWN DEVICES, IT'S LIKELY THAT HE'LL ENCOUNTER A *REAL* VILLAIN. ONE WITH VIOLENT INTENTIONS.
I KNOW HE IS, AND THAT'S THE PROBLEM!
CALL HIM UP, AND GET HIM OVER HERE RIGHT NOW.
OTHERWISE, WE'LL HAVE TO TAKE HIM IN BY FORCE.
MOYURU– CALL KOICHI FOR ME.
SO BE IT.
...

"WAKE-UP CALL" ...?
BEEP
AH... R-RIGHT.
HE'D BETTER NOT BE SLEEPING.
GIVE HIM A WAKE-UP CALL.
Y-YIKES!
AND THAT MEANS YOU GOTTA HAUL ASS AND LIE LOW UNTIL I CAN CONTACT YOU AGAIN.
IF YOU HEAR A WAKE-UP ALARM RINGTONE COMING FROM THAT PHONE, IT MEANS WE'VE GOT AN EMERGENCY.
LISTEN UP, KOICHI.
FLIP FLIP
WHOA!
RRRING
ZOO
SH
!!

WAIT!
AFTER HIM!
HALF OF YOU, WITH ME!
YOU AGREEING TO GUARD THE HOSPITAL IS WHY WE'RE COOPERATING.
YOUR MEN ARE HERE ON A SECURITY DETAIL.
Hey, you flatfoots think you can catch me?
S-sorry 'bout him.
I KNOW THAT!
...YOU MAKE A TERRIBLE NEGOTIATOR!
AND I MUST SAY, DETECTIVE TSUKAUCHI ...

CONTROL ROOM, HERE. READY TO DEPLOY.
IT'S TSUKAUCHI. THE OPERATION IS A GO.
THE TALKS BROKE DOWN, I TAKE IT?
ROGER THAT.
DRN!
THE GOAL OF THIS MISSION...
...IS THE CAPTURE OF THE HIGH-SPEED VILLAIN KNOWN AS...
WHRRR
... THE CRAWL-ER!
ROOM

BA
INGENIUM...
...DEPLOYED!!
TUM

MIDNIGHT

Midnight is always stylish in just the right way for the occasion, so her hero costume isn't the way it is just to please the crowds. It's a deliberate choice, stemming from her progressive sense of aesthetics. Probably.

—Furuhashi

I'm quickly running out of wardrobe ideas for Midnight's noncostumed appearances. With the draping, cape-like coat, I was trying to evoke a crisp, military-style look.

—Betten

EP. 97 - PURSUERS
WHOA!
ZUM
W-WHAT WAS THAT?
ZAP
ZOOP
WAS THAT...A GIANT COCKROACH ?!
HE'S FAST, WHO-EVER HE IS!!

DRRRRRK
NO ...
IT'S HIM! YOU KNOW THE ONE!
EP. 97 - PURSUERS
NARUHATA'S CREEPY-CRAWLY GUY!!

I SHOOK THE POLICE OFF MY TAIL, BUT...
...NOW I'M PRETTY FAR FROM THE HOSPITAL.
S-SORRY!
SKRE
GOTTA SNEAK BACK THERE WITHOUT GETTING CAUGHT.
THIS SHOULD BE FAR ENOUGH.
JUST GOTTA KEEP HIDDEN AND...
DRRR

?!
ING
RRRR!
YOU'RE MOVING AT DANGER-OUS SPEEDS!
SLOW DOWN AT ONCE!
THE CRAWL-ER!!

TURBO HERO: INGENIUM !!
SIR!
DR
CRAWLER!!
ZOO

ZOOP
SO PLEASE HALT!
...AND I'D LIKE TO TALK IT OVER.
I KNOW WHAT'S GOING ON WITH YOU...

WHAM
PWOP
WE CAN TALK HERE, LIKE THIS...

FOR YEARS, YOU'VE BEEN A FORCE FOR GOOD, HELPING PEOPLE OUT.
CRAWL-ER...
BUT NOW YOU'RE THE ONE IN DANGER...
...AND IT'S OUR TURN TO HELP YOU.
VRO
OOM

VROO
INGENIUM, SIR...
ONCE POP IS ALL BETTER, I'LL GO TO THE POLICE.
BUT FOR NOW...
WE CAN PROTECT YOU AND THE ONE YOU CARE ABOUT.
LET US DO THAT FOR YOU!
DOM
...
I'M SORRY!
CRAWLER!
BWAM

COOPERATING WITH THE HEROES AND THE COPS...?
NAH. THAT'S NOT GONNA WORK FOR US NOW.
THE GUY WE'RE UP AGAINST WORMED HIS WAY INTO THE POLICE STATION ALREADY.
SO OF COURSE HE COULD EXPLOIT THE GAPS IN THEIR CRUDDY SECURITY.
THAT'S WHY IT'S OUR JOB TO GUARD THOSE GAPS FROM THE OUTSIDE.
WE'RE BETTER OFF NOT BEING ANOTHER COG IN THE COPS' PLAN.
SO YOU'RE SAYING...
A FREE-LANCER OUTSIDE THE WHOLE SYS-TEM...
...IS THE BEST SHOT WE'VE GOT AGAINST THIS ENEMY.
SPE-CIALLY YOU, KOICHI.
WE NEED TO KEEP YOU FREE AND MOBILE.

I GOTTA BE FREE TO RUSH TO POP'S SIDE WHENEVER?
EXACTLY.
IS THAT IT?
EVEN WITH THE COPS ON YOUR TAIL...
EVEN WITH HEROES GUNNING FOR YOU...
GRRW
ALL YOU GOTTA FOCUS ON...
...IS PROTECTING POP FROM THE SHADOWS.

PLANNING TO SHAKE ME ON HIS HOME TURF?
HE'S HEADING INTO NARUHATA PROPER.
THAT'S SOMETHING WE ANTICIPATED, THOUGH.
SKREE
DASH
THE CRAWLER HAS ENTERED THE CAPTURE ZONE.
CONTROL ROOM, HERE.
LOOM
SECOND TEAM, DEPLOYING!
TMP TMP
BAM
IDATEN

GET HIM!
RAAAH
SREEE
TARGET IS AIRBORNE !!
BUM

EXPAND THE PERIMETER AND FOCUS ON PURSUIT!
REGROUP AND RE-DEPLOY!
SORRY, IDA! HE GOT AWAY!
ADDING VERTICALITY LIKE THAT TO HIS MOVES...
THE CRAWLER MIGHT BE TOO MUCH FOR TEAM IDATEN TO HANDLE.
OF COURSE... HE'S BEEN LEARNING THESE PAST FEW YEARS.
...
IT'S UP TO THEM TO FINISH THE JOB.
DRRRR!
BOOF
NINPO...

WAH ?!
SKLT
SPIRAL SPEAR HAND!!
SHNK
YIKES!
THERE... HE'S GROUNDED, AT LEAST.
FWRRL
INDEED.
THANK YOU.
UH-OH... YOU TWO...?

MY FIRST PROPER CONVERSATION...
...WITH THE UNSUNG HERO OF THE SKY EGG DISASTER...
THE CRAWLER.
NINJA HERO: EDGESHOT
FIBER HERO: BEST JEANIST
SOME ENTITY IS AFTER THE LIFE OF THAT POOR GIRL...
...AND YOU INTEND TO PROTECT HER YOURSELF.
More heavy hitters...
WE'VE BEEN INFORMED OF YOUR SITUATION.

GLINT
...YOU DOUBT THE EFFICACY OF PRO HEROES.
WHICH IS TO SAY...
TRULY... IT BRINGS ME GREAT SHAME TO KNOW THAT OUR INADEQUACY...
...HAS CAUSED SUCH SUFFERING.
...
UM, THAT'S ALL RIGHT...
GEEZ, SO POLITE.
AS IT'S COME TO THIS, ALLOW OUR SKILLS TO CLEAR YOUR MIND OF ANY DOUBT.
WE WILL WIN BACK YOUR TRUST.
EVERYONE KEEPS SAYING THAT...
WAIT, HUH?
GRRK
GRRK
BW
AH

MY CLOTHES ?!
!!
GRRK
THUD
CAPTURE COMPLETE!
IN THE PRESENCE OF MY FIBER MASTER, ANY CLOTHING BECOMES A STRAITJACKET.
HUMM
ZOOP
SKFSKFSKF

EMPLOYING HIS SLIDE AND GLIDE, EVEN WHILE BOUND!
RECK-LESS!
CATCH-ING CRADLE!
BOOF
NINPO: FISH-HOOK SNAG!
THAT FALL WILL BE FATAL!!
FWSH

YANK
AH!
FEELS LIKE...MY CLOTHES LOOSENED UP AGAIN?!
BOOF
FLAP FLAP
HE'S EVADED US.
WHEN A DESPERATE OPPONENT DOES NOT PRIORITIZE HIS OWN WELL-BEING...
...CAPTURE WITHOUT FURTHER INJURY BECOMES A CHALLENGE.
TWNG
QUITE TRUE.
FWRRL
MM-HMM...
RATHER, I SUPPOSE WE MISJUDGED HIS SHEER RESOLVE.
HE'S MORE CAPABLE THAN WE EXPECTED.
NO...

BUT AS PROS...
...EXCUSES ARE BENEATH US.
WHOOOSHH!
WEEOO WEEOO WEEOO
"EVEN WITH THE COPS ON YOUR TAIL..."
"EVEN WITH HEROES GUNNING FOR YOU..."
THOSE FAR-OFF SIRENS...
THEY MUST STILL BE LOOKING FOR ME.
SOMEHOW, I GOTTA GET BACK TO THE HOSPITAL.

"...IS PROTECTING POP FROM THE SHADOWS."
"ALL YOU GOTTA FOCUS ON..."
NOT MUCH DAYLIGHT LEFT.
WH-WHO'S THAT? WHO'S THERE?!
THEY MAY BE TOP-NOTCH PROS...
...BUT THOSE SURFACE DWELLERS AREN'T EQUIPPED FOR THE LIKES OF YOU.
SO YOU GAVE THE OTHERS THE SLIP, HUH?
CAN'T SAY I'M SUR-PRISED.

FWAP
COMBINING BUSTLING STREETS WITH THE RUINS OF THE OLD TOWN...
...THE CORNER OF OUR WORLD KNOWN AS NARUHATA IS A COMPLEX BLEND OF LIGHT AND DARKNESS.
A HOTBED OF CRIME.
IN OTHER WORDS ...
THE DOMAIN OF VILLAINY.
...MY HUNTING GROUNDS.
GET IT, CRAWLER ?
ERASURE HERO: ERASER HEAD

The BAD BOYS in "WHAT-IF" WORLD

THE RUFFIANS, AS SIDEKICKS.

ILLUSTRATION: BETTEN COURT

EP. 98 - IRRATIONAL PERSUASION TECHNIQUE

It's, uh...
...been a while, Eraser... sir...

CRAWLER.

THAT'S TOO FAR AWAY FOR A PROPER CONVO. COME CLOSER.
NAW, I'M GOOD. I CAN HEAR YOU FROM HERE.

WHHP!

FINE.
FLAP
!!
THEN LISTEN UP.
INGENIUM...
EDGESHOT ...
ALL THOSE PROMINENT TOP HEROES HAVE COME TO THIS PART OF TOWN FOR YOUR SAKE.
DO YOU GET THAT?
BEST JEANIST ...
THEY'RE BEING UNDERSTANDING ABOUT THE POSITION YOU'RE IN AND THE ACTIONS YOU'VE TAKEN.
YOU MIGHT EVEN SAY THEY'RE ON YOUR SIDE.
YOUR SAFETY IS WHY THEY'RE HERE.
NOT WHAT I MEAN.
I'M TALKING ABOUT THE REASON WHY.
UM, YEAH. REAL OBLIGED.

"THE SKY EGG KID"...
...IS REAL POPULAR, YOU KNOW?
TH-THANKS ...?
BUT IT'S IRRATIONAL.
YANK
KRK
KRK
GUYS LIKE YOU DON'T STOP AND REFLECT ON THEIR ACTIONS UNTIL SOME BONES GET BROKEN.
WON'T DO YOU ANY GOOD TO CODDLE YOU.
KRAK

BWAH
...HE'LL COME AT ME FOR REAL, PROBABLY!
IF I DON'T COME QUIETLY...
BUT...
...TO GET ME TO SURRENDER.
HE'S... MAKING THESE THREATS...
MY SLIDE AND GLIDE'S... NOT WORKING ?!
SKF SKF
SHAHH
FWRL
TMP

PASH!
PASH!
I APOLOGIZE!
WATCH WHERE YER GOING, CRULLER!
WAIT, WHY'S HE RUNNING ALL NORMAL-LIKE?!
EEK!
AH, SO SORRY!
WHOA!
SORRY!
FMP FMP
HEY, AIN'T THAT...
...THAT ONE HERO FROM AROUND HERE ...?
HAVEN'T SEEN HIM IN FOREVER.
FOOM
OH?

ZRM
WHAT'D HE GO BY, AGAIN...?
OOPS, SORRY...
SHUN
...'BOUT THAT.
ZRM
ZRM
I GOTTA SAY...
LOTTA ODDBALLS AROUND TOWN TODAY...
ZRM
ZRM
ZRM

THAT'S WHAT THE HOTTAS TOLD ME, WAY BACK WHEN.
HOTTA BROS.
?
FREEZE
?
IF HE LOOKS AT YOU, YOUR QUIRK STOPS WORKING.
START
ERASER'S QUIRK IS ERASURE.

MY QUIRK'S BACK IN ACTION!
IRN

...I GOTTA MOVE WHILE KEEPING OUTTA HIS LINE OF SIGHT.
FWP

SO THAT MEANS ...
IHTR
IHTR

...AND HIDING IN HIS BLIND SPOTS.
STAYING IN THE SHADOWS...
TMP

I SHOULD BE ABLE TO SHAKE HIM THAT WAY.

I'LL SNEAK FROM ALLEY TO ALLEY.
SHOOP

OR SO I THOUGHT...
FWSH
HE CUT ME OFF?!
OH. DUH. HE USED TO DO HERO WORK IN THIS AREA.
MY SHORT-CUTS AREN'T SO SECRET!
SO HE'S GOT NO PROBLEM DIVING INTO THESE ALLEYS.
FWAH

KAKLANG
MASTER'S GRAPPLING HOOK!
ZWSH
WHUP
FWP

TWICE THAT, THE CRAWLER...
ZOOM

THAT'S TWICE, NOW.
FWOO

FSHH

...WAS UNFAZED BY MY ERASURE...
...AND SWITCHED RIGHT OVER TO QUIRKLESS MANEUVERS, WITHOUT THE SLIGHTEST HESITATION.
FWAH
TMP TMP TMP

...BEFORE ANOTHER BIG ESCAPE!
BOOM
...SO HE CAN HIDE AGAIN...
HE'S CAPABLE OF PLAYING KEEP-AWAY WITH HIS NORMAL BODY...
SLAM
HUM
SHIT SHIT SHIT
THIS GUY...
GRP
THIS KID...
...IS ONE TOUGH CUS-TOMER!

THIS IS TEAM IDATEN CONTROL.
THE CRAWLER IS CURRENTLY ON THE RUN NEAR THE NARUHATA STATION DISTRICT.

ERASER HEAD IS ALREADY IN PURSUIT, AND...

INGENIUM & TEAM IDATEN SQUAD #2
Team
...THE OTHER HEROES ARE CLOSING IN.
BEST JEANIST & EDGESHOT

ROGER THAT.
KEEP ME UPDATED.

KUGISAKI ?

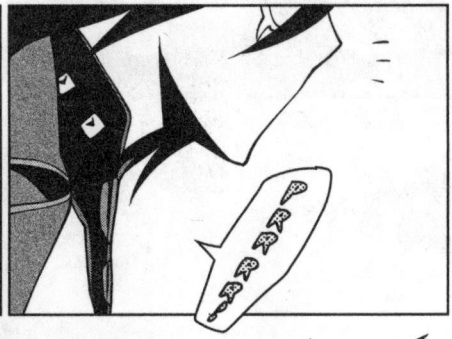
PAPAPA!

PUT THE FLATFOOT ON THE LINE.

WHERE ARE YOU?
IS THAT SOGA KUGISAKI?

...I WASN'T COUNTING ON YOU SICCING A WHOLE PACK OF BIG SHOT HEROES ON HIM.
I WAS PLANNING TO NEGOTIATE ONCE KOICHI MADE A CLEAN GETAWAY, BUT...
HEY.
SORRY FOR GIVING YOU THE SLIP BEFORE, DETECTIVE.
THIS IS TSUKAUCHI SPEAKING.
ARE YOU SAYING... HE'S WILLING TO TURN HIMSELF IN?
BUT WHAT'S THE SENSE IN DRAGGING OUT THIS PISSING CONTEST ANY LONGER?
SEEMS TO ME HIS HEAD'S WORTH A WHOLE LOT TO YOU.
THERE'S ZERO POINT TO THIS WHOLE CAT AND MOUSE CHASE.
CALL OFF YOUR DOGS.
THE OPPO-SITE.

I DON'T KNOW IF THIS IS YOUR IDEA OF HAGGLING ...
ALL WE WANT IS TO GUARD THE HOSPITAL.
...AND I CERTAINLY DON'T FEEL OBLIGATED TO SEE THINGS YOUR WAY.
IF THAT'S SUCH A CRIME, THEN LET US PAY FOR IT LATER, WHEN ALL'S SAID AND DONE.
I'M ASKING YOU TO ADJUST YOUR GAME PLAN JUST A LITTLE BIT.
HE'S... UNAVAIL-ABLE RIGHT NOW.
THAT OTHER COP... TANUMA, RIGHT?
I BET HE'D BE WILLING TO MEET IN THE MIDDLE.
THAT'S GIVING THE ENEMY EXACTLY WHAT HE WANTS.
WHICH'S THE ONLY REASON I'M TELLING YOU TO MAKE THE RIGHT CALL.
WHAT'S THE POINT OF US BEING AT EACH OTHER'S THROATS?

CORRECTA-MUNDO.
WELL, SOGA'S NOT THE PERFECT LITTLE ANGEL HE PRETENDS TO BE, BUT YES...
THE HEROES, THE COPS ...
...ARE TOO BUSY TRIPPING EACH OTHER UP TO REALIZE THEY SHOULD BE ALLIES.
...AND THE VIGILAN-TES...

EXACTLY.
THE KEY TO EVERY-THING IS TEAMWORK.
WITH SO MANY TOP HEROES RUNNING AROUND NARUHATA...
...THIS PLACE IS THE PERFECT ARENA FOR A TEST-DRIVE.
YOUR BODY'S BEEN GRANTED THE ABILITY TO DO JUST THAT.
PREVENT YOUR ENEMIES FROM TEAMING UP...
...AND ENSURE THAT YOUR OWN SIDE IS ON THE SAME PAGE.
AS YOU WISH, MASTER. ♪
IT'S TIME TO BEGIN, NUMBER 6.
DEMON-STRATE YOUR ABILITY.
SKREEE

NOOM

KRAKAM

THAT'S WHAT FINALLY KICKED IT ALL OFF.
SHAH
ZRM ZRM
THE CRAWLER'S FINAL BATTLE, THAT IS.
ONCE IT WAS ALL OVER, THEY CAME UP WITH A NAME FOR THE EVENTS OF THAT DAY.

NIGHT-
MARE
NIGHT.
FOOM

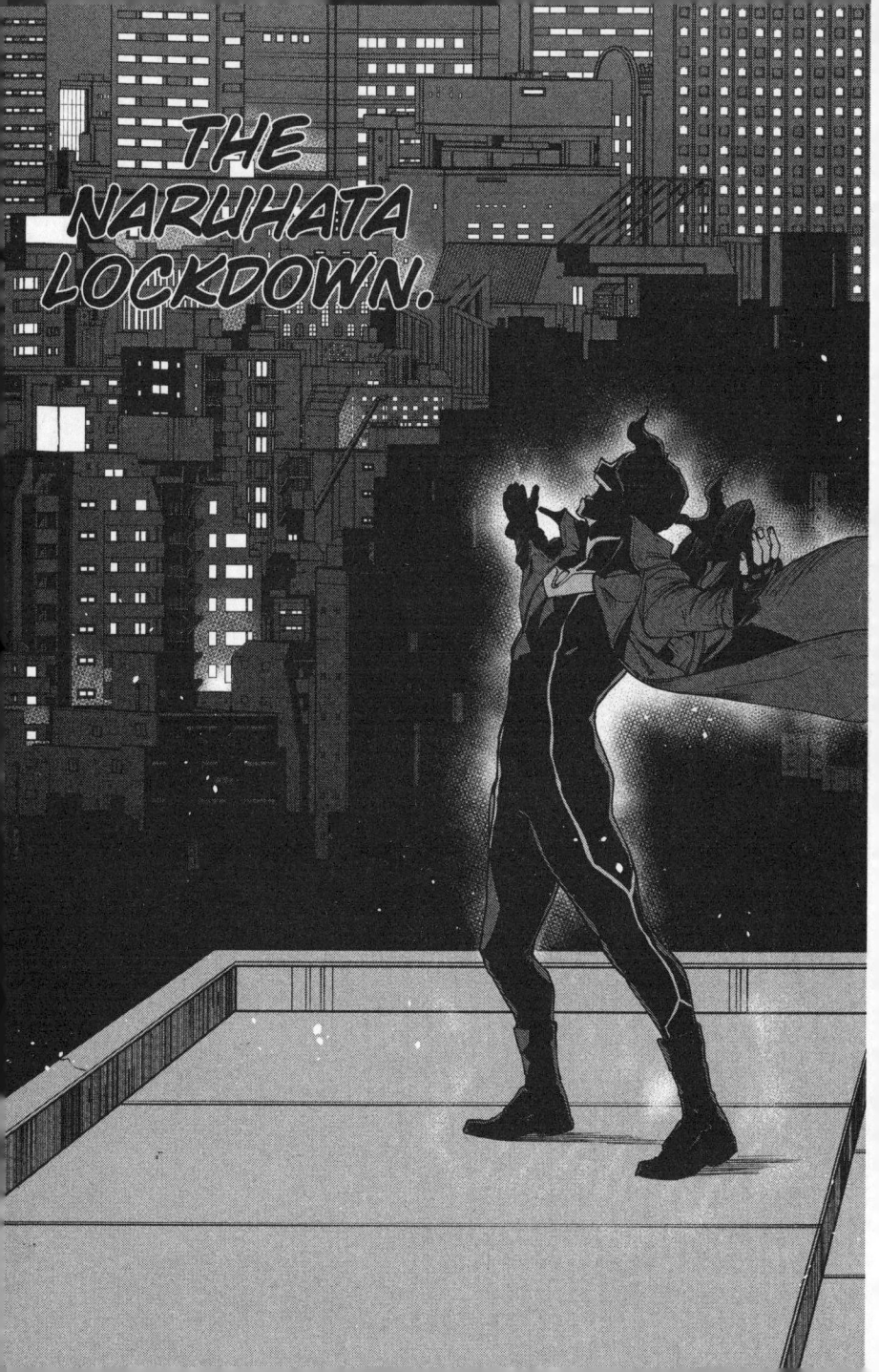
THE NARUHATA LOCKDOWN.

THE EXPLANATION

The subsequent Ep. 94.5 fills up the remaining pages in this book, and it felt like the perfect opportunity to consolidate and recap everything so far about the villainous plot and the vigilantes' heroics.

Everyone involved worked pretty hard on this.

For the good guys and bad guys alike, it's all coming to a head in this big battle. Study up before volume 13 drops!

—Furuhashi

EP. 94.5 - TANUMA'S REPORT

EP. 94.5 - TANUMA'S REPORT

Drug Trafficking and Quirk Rampage Cases

It all began with a new Quirk-enhancing drug called Trigger. The circulation of this drug was responsible for the rash of Quirk rampages that occurred in Naruhata between two and three years ago.

Previous investigations approached these events as localized, isolated incidents, but the investigation going forward will take a holistic approach and view them as links in a greater chain of scattered drug cases that plagued the nation in the past.

The following report compiles existing information on the villains connected to the events in Naruhata, in more or less chronological order.

Rash of Instant Villains (Naruhata, Tokyo)

Quirk-Enhancer Trigger

Underground Masquerade Case (Super Minami District, Osaka)

Instant Villains

"Instant villain" is the colloquial term for a person charged with Quirk-related crimes who has no previous offenses on record. These individuals do not meet the legal standards to be deemed typical villains.

Many exhibited abrupt and powerful manifestations of their Quirks via the Quirk-enhancing drug Trigger and were indistinguishable from law-abiding citizens beforehand. They also became agitated and confused when drugged. Few committed crimes that were in any way premeditated.

Charges were typically dropped in the aftermath, and these individuals were then regarded as victims within the greater drug case.

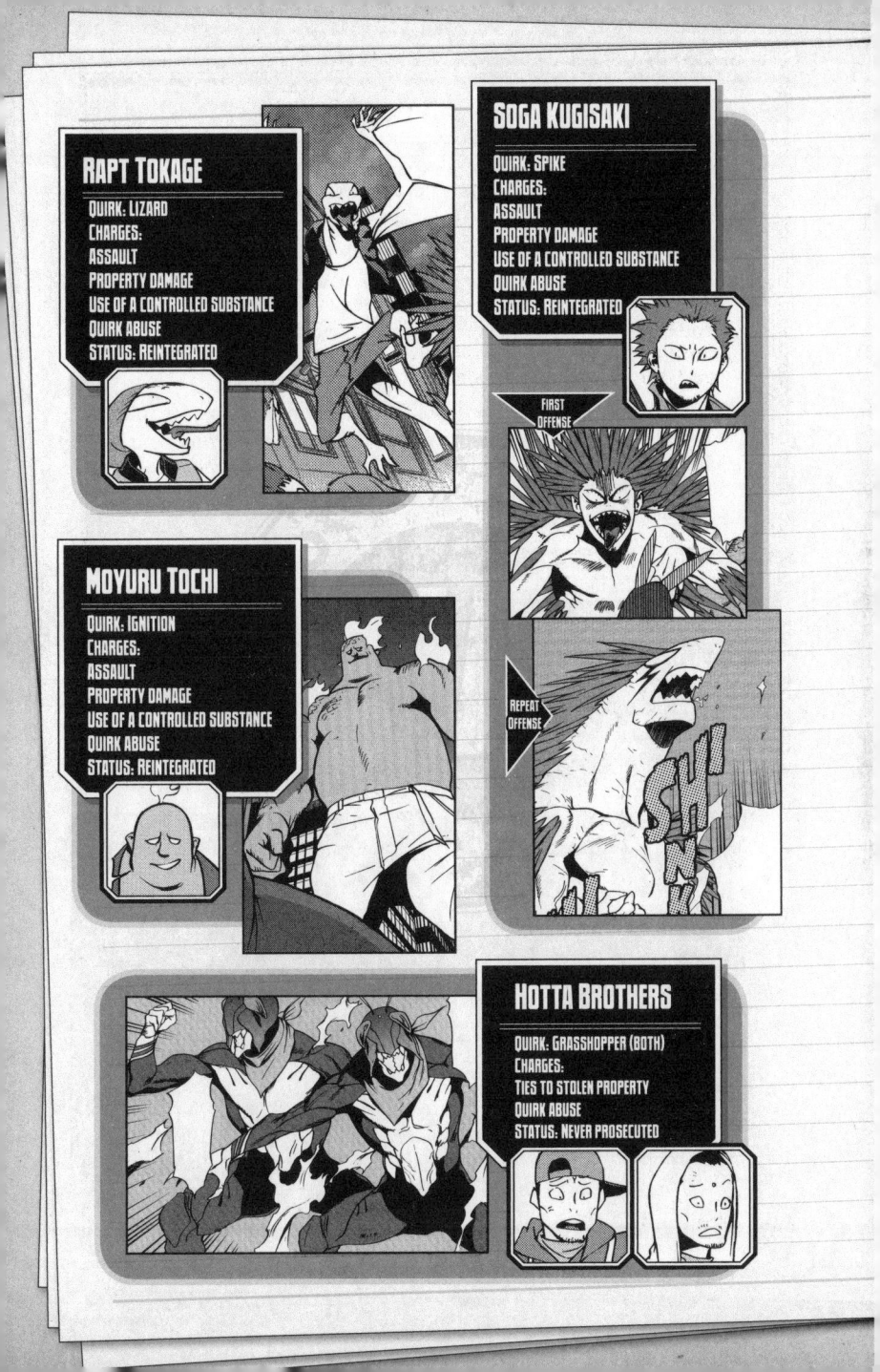
RAPT TOKAGE
QUIRK: LIZARD
CHARGES:
ASSAULT
PROPERTY DAMAGE
USE OF A CONTROLLED SUBSTANCE
QUIRK ABUSE
STATUS: REINTEGRATED
SOGA KUGISAKI
QUIRK: SPIKE
CHARGES:
ASSAULT
PROPERTY DAMAGE
USE OF A CONTROLLED SUBSTANCE
QUIRK ABUSE
STATUS: REINTEGRATED
FIRST OFFENSE
REPEAT OFFENSE
SHI
SHI
MOYURU TOCHI
QUIRK: IGNITION
CHARGES:
ASSAULT
PROPERTY DAMAGE
USE OF A CONTROLLED SUBSTANCE
QUIRK ABUSE
STATUS: REINTEGRATED
HOTTA BROTHERS
QUIRK: GRASSHOPPER (BOTH)
CHARGES:
TIES TO STOLEN PROPERTY
QUIRK ABUSE
STATUS: NEVER PROSECUTED

Supermassive Villains

Some among the instant villains manifested extreme versions of their gigantification Quirks and proceeded to rampage.

Taking into consideration the property damage caused in urban areas, these incidents rose beyond crimes to the level of bona fide disasters. Responses employing standard law enforcement tactics and ordinary heroes typically proved to be insufficient.

Several of the incidents that took place in Naruhata were resolved by pro hero Eraser Head (with his Quirk-nullifying Quirk) and the powerful American hero Captain Celebrity. Nevertheless, the neighborhood experienced significant damage to its infrastructure.

Mario Kugutsu

Quirk: Playtime
Charges:
Property destruction, Distribution of a controlled substance, Use of a controlled substance, Quirk abuse
Status: Incarcerated

Tanuma's REPORT

RYUICHI GOJIYAMA

QUIRK: KAIJU
CHARGES:
PROPERTY DESTRUCTION
USE OF A CONTROLLED SUBSTANCE
QUIRK ABUSE
STATUS: REINTEGRATED

NO IMAGE

EIJI OKAMEDA

QUIRK: GIGANTIC SPINNING FLYING TURTLE
CHARGES:
PROPERTY DESTRUCTION
USE OF A CONTROLLED SUBSTANCE
QUIRK ABUSE
STATUS: REINTEGRATED

NO IMAGE

RIKIYA ENO

QUIRK: BIG MONKEY
CHARGES:
PROPERTY DESTRUCTION
USE OF A CONTROLLED SUBSTANCE
QUIRK ABUSE
STATUS: REINTEGRATED

NO IMAGE

Remodeled Villains

A more specialized breed of instant villain that began appearing when the initial rash of Quirk rampage cases in Naruhata began to abate.

These individuals exhibit large bodies and emphasized traits of their Quirks. These changes did not come about naturally, however, but were the result of a physical remodeling process performed on each subject over a period of several months (during which each was missing).

When the remodeled villains appeared, they had been given a large dose of the Quirk-enhancing drug, making them stronger and more violent than the average villain.

Individuals had no memories from the time of their remodeling up through their respective rampages, so most were treated as victims and rehabilitated in the aftermath. But the drastic and lasting physical transformations presented many with difficulties integrating back into society.

Teruo Unagisawa

Quirk: Eel
Charges:
Property damage
Use of a controlled substance
Quirk abuse
Status: Rehabilitated

Batto Yobayakawa

Quirk: Bat
Charges:
Reckless locomotion
Use of a controlled substance
Quirk abuse
Status: Incarcerated

NO IMAGE

Tanuma's REPORT

KIRIHITO KAMACHI
QUIRK: MANTIS
CHARGES:
ASSAULT
PROPERTY DAMAGE
USE OF A CONTROLLED SUBSTANCE
QUIRK ABUSE
STATUS: REHABILITATED
RAW
RAW
RAW
WAHH
TOMMY S. GORDON
QUIRK: TANK ENGINE
CHARGES:
RECKLESS LOCOMOTION
USE OF A CONTROLLED SUBSTANCE
QUIRK ABUSE
STATUS: REHABILITATED
NO IMAGE
IKAJIRO TAKOBE
QUIRK: OCTOPUS (SQUID)
CHARGES:
ASSAULT
PROPERTY DAMAGE
USE OF A CONTROLLED SUBSTANCE
QUIRK ABUSE
STATUS: REHABILITATED
NO IMAGE
WILLY WANDA
QUIRK: DIESEL ENGINE
CHARGES:
RECKLESS LOCOMOTION
USE OF A CONTROLLED SUBSTANCE
QUIRK ABUSE
STATUS: REHABILITATED
NO IMAGE

Bomber Villains

Large villains with confirmed appearances in the Naruhata downtown area three years ago at the end of the year, and then again three months later, during the Sky Egg incident.

Dubbed "bomber villains" for convenience's sake, these entities possess Quirks enabling both flight and explosions. Individuals meeting these parameters do not exist in the official Quirk registry, so the bomber villains' identities are unknown.

These villains should be regarded as highly dangerous, as they exhibit zero sense of self-preservation and will not hesitate to perform suicide bomber attacks. Some are also capable of rapid cellular regeneration, which allows them to grow larger and perform fission.

Tanuma's REPORT

EMP BOMBER
QUIRKS: FLIGHT, DETONATION, RADIO WAVES
CHARACTERISTICS:
CAN LET LOOSE AN ELECTROMAGNETIC PULSE THAT DISABLES ALL ELECTRONICS WITHIN RANGE.
MULTIARMED VILLAIN
QUIRKS: FLIGHT, DETONATION, REGENERATION
CHARACTERISTICS:
UNLEASHES A BARRAGE OF PUNCHES. ITS FISTS EXPLODE AND REGENERATE.
CLUSTER BOMBER
QUIRKS: FLIGHT, DETONATION, PROPAGATION
RELEASES ABOUT 200 MINIATURE BOMBERS FROM WITHIN ITS BODY ALL AT ONCE.
RMBLRMBLRMBL

Coordinators

It is now reasonable to assume that some sort of organization is behind the continuous efforts to research and experiment with Quirk amplification, all of which led to the creation and deployment of the instant villains and supermassive villains (created via distribution of the Quirk-enhancing drug), as well as the remodeled villains and artificial villains.

Previous stages of the investigation treated the "Underground Masquerade," "Villain Factory," and others as separate cases, though it has become apparent that the full picture is not yet visible.

The inner workings of this organization are still relatively unknown, but at least two individuals are known to have had some degree of control over these ongoing, interconnected events.

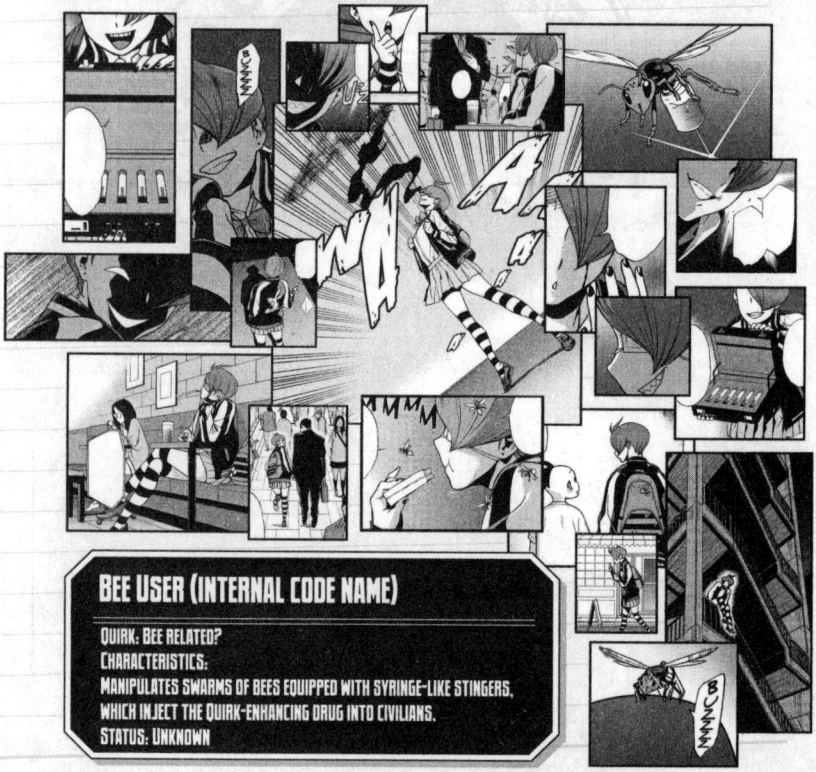

Bee User (Internal Code Name)

Quirk: Bee Related?
Characteristics:
Manipulates swarms of bees equipped with syringe-like stingers, which inject the Quirk-enhancing drug into civilians.
Status: Unknown

Tanuma's REPORT

SCARRED MAN (INTERNAL CODE NAME)
QUIRK: ACCELERATION?
CHARACTERISTICS:
KNOWN TO HAVE INFILTRATED VARIOUS LOCATIONS WHILE IN DISGUISE, EITHER TO DEPLOY REMODELED VILLAINS OR TO DESTROY INCRIMINATING EVIDENCE.
STATUS: UNKNOWN
OOH
TAP TAP TAP TAP
ZOOM
FOOOO
TOSS
HOP
FWP
BLAM
BLAM
BLAM
BLAM
BLAM
BLAM
BLAM
BLAM
FWP

"EVERY CASE SEEMS TO BE CONNECTED, BEHIND THE SCENES...
THIS READS LIKE A CONSPIRACY THEORY.
...THOUGH WE STILL HAVEN'T CONNECTED THE DOTS."
UP AGAINST SUCH A SHREWD ENEMY...
...OUR BEST MOVE WOULD BE TO...
THE HEROES HAVE ARRIVED FOR THE UPCOMING JOINT OPERATION.
DETECTIVE?
GOOD. I'LL BE RIGHT THERE.
FLICK
WHAP
IGILANTES
esponding to threats by shadowy organizations that thread
edle of the gray zone of Quirk society, official institutions
ound to come up short.
ad, unofficial peacekeeping groups intimately
ality—also known as vigilantes—are
zones themselves, respond
ion at the grassroots

VIGILANTES

When responding to threats by shadowy organizations that thread the needle of the gray zone of Quirk society, official institutions are bound to come up short.

On the other hand, unofficial peacekeeping groups intimately familiar with a given locality—also known as vigilantes—are better able to navigate those gray zones themselves, respond quickly to incidents, and procure information at the grassroots level.

Naturally the efforts of vigilantes cannot be officially condoned, but I see their existence as a sort of necessary evil. I believe that keeping them on a generous leash while maintaining a cooperative relationship could be an effective measure against the villainous organization in question.

*"Fight fire with fire." — Note that this is not the department's official stance, of course.

A HERO?

There are grander matters too, like what does it mean to be the ultimate hero in this particular world? What sort of person would that be? Those are questions and themes we'll leave to Deku, over in the main series. Meanwhile, one of the big themes in *Vigilantes* is what's the deal with plain-old Good Samaritans who aren't acting out of self-interest at all?

Plenty of people are motivated to act for the good of society, but the vast majority call it quits if that would involve breaking any rules or laws. Once in a while, you'll get someone who just goes for it anyway. I don't know if we should call that person a Good Samaritan or a criminal, but in any case, that's the story I've set out to tell.

Nevertheless, most rules exist for a reason, and breaking them arbitrarily is bound to lead to consequences. At this point, Pop and Koichi are currently facing the consequences of their actions.

How will they land, when it's all over? If you want to find out, please join me for the final few volumes.

—Hideyuki Furuhashi April 2021

Afterword

WHAT IS A HERO

is someone who helps people and battles evil. At least, that's the general image we have.

Strictly speaking, battling evil is usually for the good of society, so we could boil down the definition to "someone who fights for the good of people and society." Typically, we wouldn't call someone a hero if they're fighting for personal gain. However...

In the world of *MHA*, only professional heroes are recognized as heroes at all, so technically, every official hero performs heroics for personal gain. On the other hand, the series has introduced the notion that career heroes are not *true heroes*, and the public's faith in the pros is often shaken. As such, we once again have to ask ourselves how to define a hero. What is a hero's raison d'être?

Message from KOHEI HORIKOSHI

MY HERO ACADEMIA
Team-Up Missions

Story and Art by Yoko Akiyama
Original Concept by Kohei Horikoshi

The aspiring heroes of **MY HERO ACADEMIA** *team up with pro heroes for action-packed missions!*

BOKU NO HERO ACADEMIA TEAM UP MISSION © 2019 by Kohei Horikoshi, Yoko Akiyama/SHUEISHA Inc.

MY HERO ACADEMIA SMASH!!

Story and Art by Hirofumi Neda
Original Concept by Kohei Horikoshi

HILARIOUS HIJINKS
featuring the characters and story lines of
MY HERO ACADEMIA!

The superpowered society of *My Hero Academia* takes a hilarious turn in this reimagining of the best-selling series! Join Midoriya, All Might and all the aspiring heroes of U.A. High, plus memorable villains, in an irreverent take on the main events of the series, complete with funny gags, ridiculous jokes and superpowered humor!

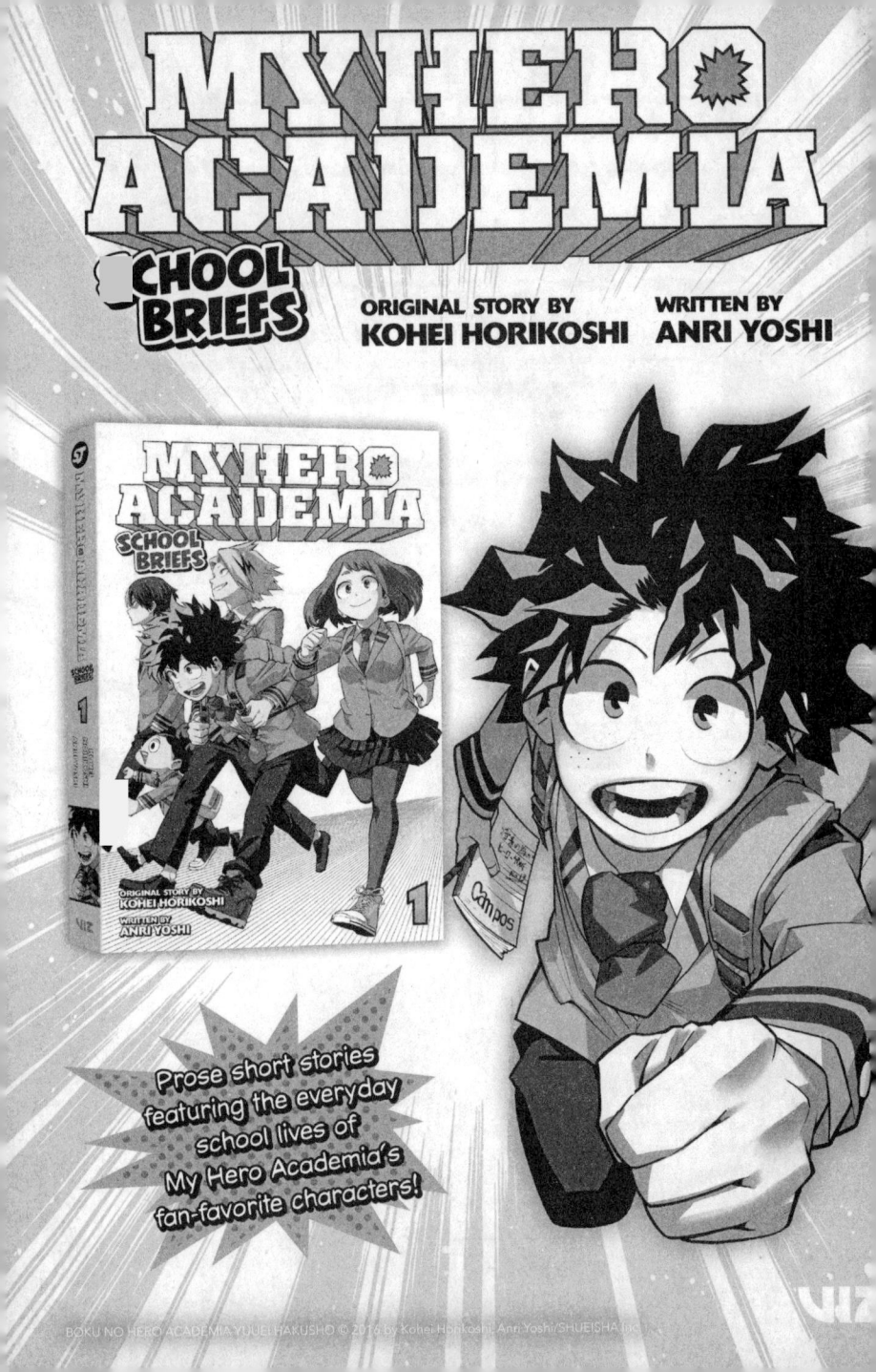

BOKU NO HERO ACADEMIA YUUEI HAKUSHO © 2014 by Kohei Horikoshi/ Anri Yoshi/SHUEISHA Inc.

YOU'RE READING THE WRONG WAY!!
MY HERO ACADEMIA VIGILANTES
reads from right to left, starting in the upper-right corner. Japanese is read from right to left, meaning that action, sound effects, and word-balloon order are completely reversed from English order.
4
3
2
1
2
1
8
7
6
5
4
3
9
5
142

CAN MUSCLES CRUSH MAGIC?!

MASHLE

MAGIC AND MUSCLES

STORY AND ART BY
HAJIME KOMOTO

In the magic realm, magic is everything—everyone can use it, and one's skill determines their social status. Deep in the forest, oblivious to the ways of the world, lives Mash. Thanks to his daily training, he's become a fitness god. When Mash is discovered, he has no choice but to enroll in magic school where he must beat the competition without revealing his secret—he can't use magic!

MASHLE © 2020 by Hajime Komoto/SHUEISHA Inc.

RATED T TEEN
VIZ